The
Gold Medal
FONDUE
Cookbook

The
Gold Medal
FONDUE
Cookbook

Marie Roberson Hamm

A FAWCETT GOLD MEDAL BOOK

Fawcett Publications, Inc., Greenwich, Conn.

Acknowledgments

To RITA KUPKA and to her great talent for preparing good food and her never-failing good taste

To PAT COLEINE for her everlasting patience, sense of organization, and fine precision

Contents

6   *Golden Cheese Fondues*

7 Meat, Poultry, Fish, and Other Fondues

10   CONTENTS

8   Sauces Add to the Fun

9   Bread for Fondues

12   CONTENTS

10   Dip into Desserts

The
Gold Medal
FONDUE
Cookbook

1

*Fondue
Is Not New
(But It's Better than Ever)*

The original ancestor of Swiss fondue was born of necessity. Bread and cheese, made in the summer, lasted until spring, both hardening as the cold snow-bound winter set in, until the bread was "sliced" into chunks with an ax. To make it palatable, a large piece of cheese was scraped and heated near the fire until it softened to a creamy mass. Chunks of bread were dipped into the saucy cheese and became an edible treat. This was called *raclette*, meaning "a scraping."

Subsequently a refinement of melting shredded or diced cheese in hot wine for the bread dip became known as *fondue*, a noun derived from the French verb *fondre*, which means "to melt."

The cheese-wine sauce with bread dip is the true fondue. However, other countries had parallel cooking ideas. The oriental "hot pots," pots of broth or oil heated on charcoal table stoves with cylinders for charcoal, were communal family receptacles in which pieces of meats and vegetables were cooked in a leisurely manner and served with rice. The broth left after cooking was then served as soup in cups.

The Borgias, those unpleasant players in the drama of the Italian Renaissance, employed the method of dipping food in one pot with guests, to insure their friendship—for who would poison a dish from which he himself was feasting?

Later in Italy it was *Fritto Misto*, an imaginative meal of many foods. The tidbits were coated in batter which enclosed all the nourishing qualities and flavors of the foods as they were quickly cooked in hot oil.

It was inevitable that the imagination of the Chinese, Italian, and French chefs carried the fondue idea into a world of variation. Meats, fish, poultry, and vegetables were brought to the scene and alternately cooked in hot oil or boiling broth at the "roundtable."

The first dessert fondue is said to have originated in a Swiss restaurant in New York City. The recipe called for a tempting hot chocolate sauce in which cubes of cake were dunked. When the dessert became a "public property," fruits, nuts, and other sweet bits were added to the dunkable list.

And so in the age of Aquarius, fondue has come to mean foods that are heated or cooked or dunked into liquid in a fondue or other adequate pot. Definitively, there are two types: those in which pieces of bread, cake, fruits, and other foods are dipped into hot sauces until coated; and those in which tidbits are plunged into and cooked in hot oil or liquid.

Fondue is a culinary game for young partiers, skiers and winter sportsmen, vacationers, and for all the young at heart. It pleases men as much if not perhaps a little bit more than women. Any time of the day or night is the right time for a fondue.

If dunking should turn out to be the most popular American pastime, we'll have the happiest state in the universe. This pleasurable, companionable eating game levels all company to a state of euphoria—laughs and friendship are inescapable. Who can resist the urge to DUNK? Queens do it. Peasants do it. Behind the scenes even the most frightening butlers do it. So who can resist the fun of dunking his merry way through a fondue meal?

2

Fondue
Pots and Equipment

As in other specialty cooking, there is a handsome choice of fondue equipment. In the stores you will find a good selection of enameled cast iron or aluminum pots in a number of colors, as well as satiny stainless steel or lined copper or brass for all-round use, and thick earthenware dishes for the saucy dessert fondues.

Over in the electric appliance department, you'll discover several brands of efficient electric pots with automatic controls.

A new electric automatic fondue has a thermostatic control that maintains the correct heat for all kinds of fondue and tempura cooking, without scorching, smoking, or burning. Cooking oil stays at the "just right" temperature without adjustment; a signal light blinks to indicate proper temperature maintenance. The "double boiler" effect prevents scorching of cheese, chocolate, and cream fondues. A top tray with rack holds foods to be warmed, and drain slots make it easy to add more water without disturbing the center bowl, while providing drainage of foods cooked in liquid. Eight color-coded fondue forks fit into slots in the base of the automatic fondue.

Forks are important implements in fondue cooking. You'll want them to be long enough to reach into the pot with plenty of clearance, about 10 inches long. The prongs should be long and sharp so they will penetrate and hold the bread, meat, or whatever. The handles must be heatproof. When cooking in hot oil, it is a good idea to also have dinner forks, since the prongs of the cooking fork could burn lips or tongue. Inexpensive wooden skewers, about 8 to 10 inches long may substitute for fondue forks.

A tray about 9 to 12 inches is esssential to place under the pot to protect the table from spattering or dripping. A washable mat will serve the same purpose.

There are special fondue plates, often matching the enamelware fondue pot colors. These have divisions or separate sections for meat and sauces.

On the other hand, you may have just the thing for a fondue cook-in on your own kitchen shelf. A chafing dish is a good choice for cheese or dessert fondues, since it can be set over water so the sauce stays at an even controlled heat. An electric skillet gives a good performance as a fondue cooker with the advantage of easy-to-set controls.

You can improvise with a saucepan over an electric hot plate (although you may find the heating unit a bit hard to control). Dessert fondue sauce is quite easy to prepare in a saucepan or double boiler at a range and then transfer to a casserole or fondue pot, to keep hot but not cooking, over a candle warmer.

To help you decide which unit to buy, let's go over the points you'll want to consider at the time of purchase. The most expensive choice is not necessarily the best nor the right one for you— you may not need all the features it offers. However, an unusually low price may be an indication of poor quality. If you want a designer's color, the popular enamelware pots with trays are the answer. They're efficient, fairly easy to clean, and all-purpose. For a modern setting you might want a classic stainless steel unit with the same qualities as enamelware. The cordon bleu gourmet will

select a copper or brass pot with a metal lining—
a touch more trouble to keep bright and shiny, but
worth the effort.* If you plan to specialize in
dessert fondues, you'll want the thick earthenware casserole with a plump handle, especially
designed for keeping sweet sauces hot over low
spirit or candle flames.

*Check the lining—you'll want it to be either stainless
steel or a heavy tin plate.

3

**The
Fondue
Flame or Heat**

Burners which may be regulated to keep each type of fondue cooking at the desired heat are important. Some electric units have automatic controls. Alcohol and sterno burners can be regulated by lengthening or shortening wicks and by opening or closing the burner lid. Electric, alcohol, and sterno units produce the most heat and are good for cooking meat, fish, and other foods in hot fat. They can also be regulated for use with all the slower-cooking cheese and dessert fondues.

Candle warmers are effective for dessert fondues where the sauce, which is initially cooked at the range, is merely kept hot over the candle flame.

Cheese fondues require medium heat, or just enough to keep the sauce fluid but not boiling; oil or fat and broth fondues require enough heat to keep the liquid at a slow-rolling but not smoking boil.

4

How
Do You
Do Fondues?

From experience I have found that the easiest method of heating cheese, oil, or cooking sauces is at the range. It can be done over alcohol or sterno heat, but this requires some time and patience. After heating the sauce or liquid at the range, quickly transfer the pot to fondue stand heat. Then regulate the heat so there is just enough to keep the contents of the pot at required cooking temperature—the cheese or sweet sauce fluid, the oil or broth at a medium rolling boil. If your fondue becomes too thick, add a small amount of the heated liquid called for in the recipe.

Pieces to be cooked or dunked should be cut into bite-size chunks—a ¾- to 1-inch cube is a good size for most morsels.

Too many cooks can spoil the fondue. A group of 4 to 6 is a comfortable number for one cooking pot. If you plan to have more guests, seat 4 to 5 of them at small tables with a fondue cooker on each. Serve sauces in cup-size bowls that are easy to pass for individual plate servings.

Practice makes perfect, as any fondue fan will tell you. Tradition holds that when a man loses a piece of bread to the bottom of the pot, he forfeits a bottle of wine to the table. When a lady has the same mishap, she pays with a kiss to each man present.

The beverage to serve with fondue can be hot tea, chilled beer, room temperature wine, or liqueurs in keeping with the kind of fondue you are serving.

Wine, candlelight, and soft music add to the magic mood. Snowy white or pastel tablecloths, crystal goblets, and a cluster of fresh flowers suggest to your guests that you are a considerate hostess with a natural flair for entertaining.

5

Fondue
Appetizers

Party people fondly remember the hostess who serves good food and does it with a special flair. A fondue pot brings conviviality to a cocktail gathering and creates a warm atmosphere that breeds friendship and produces hot bites of goodness.

When you think about it, what goes with cold drinks? Hot appetizers, of course. The fondue appetizer is a blessed release for the hostess, too. The little pot bubble-bubbles with very little toil or trouble.

Wooden skewers, chop sticks, or wooden forks with different colored handles are ideal for fondue hors d'oeuvre cooking. You'll also want to have a stack of small paper or china plates and napkins on the table.

Antipasto Fondue

1 (9-ounce) package frozen potato puffs
1 (7-ounce) package frozen miniature egg rolls
1 (7-ounce) package frozen French fried egg-
    plant
1 (6-ounce) package frozen pizza rolls
1 (6-ounce) package frozen fried shrimp
1 (4-ounce) can mushroom caps, drained
Italian Sauce*
Mustard Cream Sauce*
Tartar Sauce*
1 clove garlic
2 cups peanut oil

Beforehand Preparation

At room temperature thoroughly defrost and dry
all frozen foods; cut larger pieces into 1-inch
chunks. Drain mushroom caps; save liquid for
gravy or stews. Prepare sauces.

Tabletop Technique

Rub fondue pot with garlic. In fondue pot at
range, heat oil to bubbling. Transfer to fondue
stand over medium flame; keep oil bubbling. Each
person spears a tidbit on fondue fork or wooden
skewer, cooks it in oil for about 1 minute or until
golden brown, then dips the piece into one of the
sauces. About 10 to 12 appetizer servings.

MENU
Wine on the Rocks   Beer
Antipasto Fondue
Sauces
Coffee

*Instructions for preparing the sauces marked with an
asterisk may be found by consulting the Index.

Bagna Cauda
(A Vegetable Hors d'Oeuvre Fondue)

1 small head cauliflower
1 cucumber
1 green pepper
1 bunch celery
3 Belgian endive
1 (2-ounce) can flat anchovies
3 cloves garlic
1 loaf crusty Italian bread
¼ pound butter
¼ cup olive oil
¼ cup salad oil

Beforehand Preparation

Separate cauliflower into small flowerettes; soak in salted water for 30 minutes; drain thoroughly. Peel cucumber; cut into sticks. Slice green pepper into strips. Separate hearts of celery; cut outer stalks into sticks. Separate endive leaves. Keep vegetables crisp in refrigerator. To serve, arrange attractively on a platter of shiny leaves or lettuce. Drain anchovies; chop fine. Mash garlic. Cut bread into 1-inch cubes.

Tabletop Technique

Combine garlic, butter, and oils in fondue pot. Simmer over very low heat at range for 5 minutes; do not allow to boil. Add anchovies. Transfer to fondue stand over low heat. Using fondue forks or skewers, dip vegetables and bread cubes into hot sauce. Serves 8 to 10.

MENU
Cocktails   Bagna Cauda   Wine

Clam Dip Fondue

2 loaves French bread
¼ cup grated Parmesan cheese
1 tablespoon chopped parsley
1 tablespoon cornstarch
2 (7-ounce) cans minced clams, undrained
8 slices bacon, chopped
1 clove garlic, minced
½ cup tomato puree
½ teaspoon basil, crushed
Dash salt and pepper

Beforehand Preparation

Cut bread into crusty 1-inch cubes. Grate cheese. Chop parsley. Blend cornstarch with clams. Chop bacon. Mince garlic.

Tabletop Technique

At range in fondue pot, cook bacon until crisp. Pour off all but 1 tablespoon fat; add garlic; brown lightly. Add tomato puree, basil, salt and pepper, and clam mixture. Cook over low heat until slightly thickened; stirring constantly. Blend in cheese and parsley. Transfer to fondue stand over low flame. With fondue fork swirl bread into sauce. If mixture thickens, stir in a little warm milk. 8 to 12 servings.

DROP-IN FOR A DIP-IN MENU
Clam Dip Fondue
Mulled Cider

Cumberland Ham Fondue

1 pound cooked ham, 1-inch thick
1 (10-ounce) jar red currant jelly
1 (6-ounce) jar prepared mustard

Beforehand Preparation
Cut ham into 1-inch cubes.

Tabletop Technique
At range in fondue pot over low heat, melt jelly; add mustard. Transfer to fondue stand over low flame. Dunk ham cubes into hot sauce. 8 to 12 appetizer servings.

OPEN HOUSE MENU
Strawberry Champagne Cup
Cumberland Ham Fondue

Curried Meatballs with Beer Sauce

2 slices white bread, cubed
1 (12-ounce) can beer
1½ pounds ground beef
¼ cup minced onion
1 egg, slightly beaten
2 tablespoons ketchup
½ teaspoon salt
1 teaspoon curry powder
2 (10½-ounce) cans condensed cream of mush-
    room soup
¼ cup water
2 tablespoons chopped parsley

Beforehand Preparation

Cube bread; soak in ½ cup beer. Combine beef,
onion, egg, ketchup, salt, ½ teaspoon curry powder; add bread mixture. Mix well. Shape into 48
meatballs. Arrange in a single layer in a large
baking pan. Bake at 300°F. for about 15 minutes;
turn once. Chop parsley.

Tabletop Technique

At range in fondue pot, blend soup, water, remaining beer, and curry powder and parsley. Heat;
stir often. Transfer to fondue stand over low
flame. Dip meatballs on fondue forks into hot
sauce for about 1 minute. 48 appetizers.

SAFARI PARTY MENU

Scotch   Gin   Rum   Brandy
Cheese Crackers
Curried Meatballs with Beer Sauce
Black Coffee   Liqueurs

Franks with Beer BBQ Sauce

2 pounds frankfurters
2 cups beer
1 cup minced onion
1 cup ketchup
½ cup brown sugar
¼ cup prepared mustard
2 tablespoons Worcestershire sauce
1 teaspoon salt
¼ teaspoon pepper

Beforehand Preparation
Cut frankfurters into bite-size pieces. Allow beer to reach room temperature. Mince onion.

Tabletop Technique
In fondue pot at range, combine beer with all ingredients except frankfurters. Heat, stirring often. Simmer 10 minutes to blend flavors. Transfer to fondue stand over low flame. Dunk frankfurters into hot sauce until heated through, using fondue forks or tooth picks. About 64 appetizers.

OFF CAMPUS SIP AND SNACK-IN
Beer
Franks with Beer BBQ Sauce
Coffee

Oriental Beef Cubes

1½ pounds boneless beef sirloin, cut into ¾-inch cubes
¼ cup soy sauce
3 tablespoons sliced fresh ginger
1 clove garlic, crushed
1½ teaspoons sugar
3 to 4 small hot red chilies, seeded and crushed
Toasted sesame seeds
1½ cups peanut oil
Soy sauce

Beforehand Preparation

Cut beef into cubes. Refrigerate. Combine soy sauce, ginger, garlic, sugar, and crushed chilies. Toast sesame seeds. About 30 minutes before serving, pour soy sauce mixture over meat; stir occasionally. Remove beef cubes; drain.

Tabletop Technique

At range in fondue pot, heat oil. Transfer to fondue stand; keep oil bubbling. Using fondue fork, dip beef in hot oil, cooking until done to taste. Sprinkle with soy sauce; then dip in toasted sesame seeds. About 48 appetizers.

SAKE PARTY
Heated Sake
Oriental Beef Cubes
Tea

Pacific Hors d'Oeuvre Fondue

½ pound chicken livers
½ pound small cooked meatballs
½ pound cooked shrimp
2 tablespoons cornstarch
2 tablespoons sugar
½ cup water
⅓ cup vinegar
1 cup pineapple juice
2 tablespoons soy sauce
1 tablespoon butter
1 chicken bouillon cube

Beforehand Preparation

Cook chicken livers; cut into bite-size pieces. Prepare meatballs and shrimp.

Tabletop Technique

At range in fondue pot over low heat, combine cornstarch and sugar. Gradually add water; stir until smooth. Add remaining ingredients. Simmer 5 minutes; stir often. Transfer to fondue stand over low flame. Using fondue forks or tooth picks, dunk chicken livers, meatballs, or shrimp in hot sauce. 8 appetizer servings.

SUNDAY DROP-IN MENU
Dry White Wine   Dry Red Wine
Pacific Hors d'Oeuvre Fondue
Coffee

Pigs in Blankets Fondue

1 (8-ounce) can refrigerated crescent dinner
    rolls
2 to 3 tablespoons barbecue sauce
1 (4-ounce) can Vienna sausage
2 (14-ounce) packages frozen Swiss fondue
3 tablespoons kirsch
Dash pepper

Beforehand Preparation

Unroll and separate dough into 4 rectangles; press
all perforations to seal well. Cut each rectangle
crosswise into 6 strips. Brush with barbecue
sauce. Cut sausages crosswise into 3 pieces. Roll
dough strips around each sausage. Place seam-side
down on ungreased cookie sheet. Bake at 375°F
for 12 to 15 minutes or until golden brown.

Tabletop Technique

At range in fondue pot, prepare fondue accord-
ing to package directions. Add kirsch and pepper.
Stir until smooth. Transfer to fondue stand over
low flame. With fondue fork spear sausage roll
and swirl in fondue. About 24 appetizers.

MENU
Pigs in Blankets
Beer   Wine

Roast Beef Sandwich Fondue

8 slices buttered toast
8 thin slices cooked roast beef
Prepared horseradish
1 (10½-ounce) can condensed golden mush-
    room soup
½ soup can water

Beforehand Preparation
Top 4 slices toast with roast beef; spread with
horseradish. Cover. Cut each sandwich into bite-
size pieces.

Tabletop Technique
In fondue pot at range, blend soup and water.
Heat, stirring often. Transfer to fondue stand
over low flame. To serve, each person spears a
small sandwich and dunks it in the hot sauce.
About 36 appetizers.

BEER BARREL BONANZA
Beer
Roast Beef Sandwich Fondue
Corn Chips   Nuts   Pretzels

Scotch Woodcock Fondue

16 slices buttered toast
4 (3-ounce) packages cream cheese, softened
24 slices bacon, cooked, drained, and crumbled
1 (10¾-ounce) can condensed Cheddar cheese
    soup
1 (10¾-ounce) can condensed tomato soup
1 cup water
¼ cup dry white wine

Beforehand Preparation
Spread toast slices with cream cheese; top 8 slices with crumbled bacon. Cover with remaining toast. Cut into bite-size pieces.

Tabletop Technique
At range in fondue pot over low heat, blend soups; gradually add water and wine. Heat, stirring often. Transfer to fondue stand over low flame. With fondue fork dunk small sandwiches into hot sauce. About 72 appetizers.

SUNDAY TV SNACK
Bull Shots
Scotch Woodcock Fondue
Coffee

Shrimp and Lobster in Curry Dip

2 cups cooked, shelled, and deveined shrimp
2 cups cooked lobster meat
¼ cup chopped onion
½ cup chopped celery
1 apple, peeled and chopped
¼ cup butter
1 tablespoon curry powder
Dash salt and pepper
1½ cups tomato juice
1 tablespoon tomato paste

Beforehand Preparation

Prepare seafood; cut into bite-size pieces. Chop onion and celery. Just before serving, chop apple.

Tabletop Technique

In fondue pot at range over low heat, cook onion, celery, and apple in butter until vegetables are tender. Stir in curry powder, salt, and pepper. Add tomato juice and tomato paste; cook until slightly thickened. Transfer to fondue stand over low flame. With fondue forks or toothpicks dip lobster meat and shrimp into hot sauce. 8 to 12 appetizer servings.

HAWAIIAN COCKTAIL LUAU
Cocktails
Shrimp and Lobster in Curry Dip
Chopped Chutney   Grated Coconut
Nuts   Chopped Parsley
Coffee

South African Dip-In

8 (3-ounce) South African rock lobster tails
2 pounds tender lean beef, 1½ inches thick
1 quart red wine vinegar
1 bay leaf
1 teaspoon pepper
2 teaspoons salt
1 pound frying peppers
1½ cups peanut oil
½ cup butter
2 teaspoons aromatic bitters

Beforehand Preparation

Parboil frozen lobster tails by dropping in boiling salted water; when water reboils, drain immediately; drench with cold water. Cut away underside membrane; remove meat; slice into ½-inch pieces; arrange in shells for service. Slice steak into thin strips; marinate for 2 hours in marinade of wine vinegar, bay leaf, pepper, and salt. Cut peppers into strips.

Tabletop Technique

At range in fondue pot, heat oil, butter, and aromatic bitters to bubbling. Transfer to fondue stand over medium flame; keep bubbling hot. Guests immerse lobster, meat, or pepper in hot oil until cooked to taste, about 1 to 2 minutes, then dip into favorite sauce. Heat and add more oil as needed. Makes enough for a group of 24.

MENU
South African Dip-In
Buttered Pumpernickel Slices   Wine

Spicy Appetizer Dogs

1 (1½-ounce) package spaghetti-sauce mix
1 (8-ounce) can tomato sauce
1½ cups water
2 tablespoons salad oil
2 (6-ounce) jars cocktail wieners

Beforehand Preparation

Prepare spaghetti-sauce mix, adding tomato sauce, water, and salad oil following label directions. Drain cocktail wieners; cut each sausage in half.

Tabletop Technique

At range in fondue pot, heat spaghetti sauce. Transfer to fondue stand over low flame. Using fondue forks or long toothpicks, dunk wieners into hot sauce. About 40 appetizers.

TEEN TALK-IN
Spicy Appetizer Dogs
Soft Drinks

Tomato Cheese Fondue with Biscuit Bites

2 (8-ounce) cans refrigerated flaky baking
    powder biscuits
2 cups shredded Swiss cheese
¼ cup flour
1 (10¾-ounce) can condensed tomato soup
½ cup dry white wine
⅛ teaspoon salt
⅛ teaspoon nutmeg
Dash pepper

Beforehand Preparation

Cut each biscuit in half; place cut-side down on
ungreased cookie sheet. Bake at 400°F. for 10 to
12 minutes or until golden brown. Cut into bite-
size pieces. Shred cheese; toss with flour.

Tabletop Technique

At range in fondue pot over low heat, blend soup,
wine, salt, nutmeg, and pepper. Gradually add
cheese, stirring constantly until cheese is melted.
Transfer to fondue stand over low flame. With
fondue forks dip bite-size pieces of biscuits into
fondue. About 40 appetizers.

WINE TASTING PARTY
Red Wine   White Wine   Rosé
Oysters   Clams   Crab Chunks
Tomato Cheese Fondue with Biscuit Bites
Demitasse

Western Bean Cocktail Dip

1 (1-pound) can kidney beans, drained
1 clove garlic
1 tablespoon chopped green onion
⅛ to ¼ teaspoon hot pepper sauce
2 teaspoons Worcestershire sauce
2 tablespoons mayonnaise
Juice of 1 lemon
Tortilla chips
Corn chips

Beforehand Preparation
In blender combine all ingredients except chips.
Blend until smooth.

Tabletop Technique
At range in fondue pot, heat blended mixture.
Transfer to fondue stand over low flame. Serve
with tortilla and corn chips. About 2 cups dip.

WESTERN FONDUE DIP MENU
Western Bean Cocktail Dip
Tortilla Chips
Corn Chips
Stuffed Celery
Beer   Soft Drinks

6

*Golden
Cheese Fondues*

The Swiss agree that a chilled beverage is
de trop with cheese fondue, reasoning that it
congeals the creamy mixture before it has
a chance to be properly digested. They serve hot
tea or a glass of fiery kirsch which is sipped at
the start, the midway point, and the finale of
the fondue ritual. Room temperature wine is also
acceptable.

Mature, naturally aged bulk cheeses such as
Emmenthaler, a mild Swiss cheese, or Gruyère,
a stronger variety, or our own Cheddar, make the
best fondues, but firm process cheese can be used
with satisfactory results. Grate or finely mince
the cheese so that it melts quickly. Bring the wine
to a simmer (do not boil) before adding the
cheese, a handful at a time, and stirring smooth
after each addition with a wooden spoon. Keep
the heat low—high heat makes the cheese stringy
and difficult to handle. It should be kept at a
gentle simmer. If the sauce cools or becomes thick,
add a little warm wine, stirring in a little at a
time until the sauce returns to a dunkable consistency. A good trick is to add a spoonful of
butter with the cheese—this helps keep the sauce
from thickening. Tomato products are apt to
create a slightly grainy texture, but this does not
alter the good flavor.

The bread should be crunchy-crusty, lightly
oven-toasted, if you so choose, with a crust on one
side. The chunks should be speared toward the
crust, to keep the bread from slipping off the fork
into the fondue—heaven forbid!

In Switzerland, boiled or fried potatoes are
often substituted as a variation for bread. With
the exciting assortment in the supermarket

freezer cases, why not serve various crusty potatoes for a delicious new experience?

Experienced dunkers exercise a figure-eight
motion, swirling the morsels down to the bottom
of the pot to prevent the cheese from thickening
and sticking near the heat.

Many of the recipes in this book suggest
rubbing a clove of garlic inside the pot before
preparing the sauce. The flavorful bud is a classic
seasoner for fondues but optional for those who
shun garlic.

Cheese-coated pots can be difficult to clean;
however, an all-purpose liquid cleanser with am-
monia will dissolve the cheese without injuring
the lining of the pot.

Apple Rabbit Fondue

1 pound aged natural Cheddar cheese
1 (12-ounce) can beer
2 teaspoons dry mustard
1 teaspoon Worcestershire sauce
1 teaspoon paprika
1 teaspoon butter
6 or 8 apples
Toast chunks or triangles

Beforehand Preparation
Remove rind; grate cheese or cut into mealy pieces. Open beer; let stand for at least 1 hour at room temperature before using. Combine seasonings.

Tabletop Technique
Melt butter in fondue pot, tipping to coat bottom. Add cheese, a handful at a time, stirring with wooden spoon until each addition is melted. Gradually add 1 cup beer, stirring constantly. Stir in seasonings and continue to stir until the cheese "follows the spoon around the pan." If cheese thickens, gradually add more beer. Each guest cuts an apple into cubes and alternately dunks bread and apple chunks into the fondue. 6 to 8 servings.

MENU
Apple Rabbit Fondue
Dilled Green Bean Salad with Pimiento Garnish
Ice Cream Croquettes Rolled in
Rum-Soaked Macaroon Crumbs
Coffee   Beer

Après Ski Toddy Fondue

2 cups coffee
1 (15¼-ounce) can pineapple chunks
4 small bananas
Lemon juice
1 (8-ounce) package cream cheese, softened
⅓ cup brown sugar
6 ounces Swiss cheese, grated
¼ cup flour
1½ ounces rum

Beforehand Preparation
Prepare coffee. Drain pineapple; save juice for future use. Peel bananas, cut into 1-inch slices, brush with lemon juice. Blend cream cheese with brown sugar. Grate Swiss cheese, toss with flour.

Tabletop Technique
In fondue pot heat coffee; over medium flame gradually add grated cheese, stirring constantly until smooth after each addition. Add cream cheese mixture; stir until smooth. Just before serving, heat rum, light it, and pour over the fondue; stir it in. Fruits are speared on heat-proof fondue forks, then swirled into fondue. 4 servings.

FIRESIDE MENU
Apres Ski Toddy Fondue
Coffee with Rum

Brunch Fondue

1 pound Swiss cheese
3 tablespoons flour
½ teaspoon dry mustard
⅛ teaspoon nutmeg
¼ teaspoon ground ginger
Dash seasoned salt
4 to 6 English muffins
1 (8-ounce) package precooked pork sausages
1 cup beer
½ bunch parsley
1 cup undiluted evaporated milk

Beforehand Preparation

Shred or mince cheese; toss with flour. Combine mustard, nutmeg, ginger, and seasoned salt. Split in half and toast muffins; cut into little pie-shaped wedges. Brown sausages and cut in half. Allow beer to reach room temperature. Mince parsley.

Tabletop Technique

In fondue pot heat evaporated milk and beer to bubbling. Add cheese, a handful at a time, stirring smooth after each addition. Add mixed seasonings. Blend until smooth. With long-handled fondue forks alternately dip muffin wedges and sausage pieces into fondue. Lightly dip into parsley. 4 to 6 servings.

MENU
Brunch Fondue
Dill Pickle Slices
Hearts of Celery   Scallions
Pears Poached in Red Wine
Bloody Marys   Coffee

Champagne Fondue

1 pound Gruyère cheese
3 tablespoons flour
French bread or toasted rolls
1 clove garlic
2 cups champagne
¼ cup cognac
½ teaspoon salt
Dash of paprika or a few grains cayenne

Beforehand Preparation

Cube or grate cheese and mix well with flour. Cut bread or rolls into bite-size pieces. Peel and cut garlic clove in half.

Tabletop Technique

At range rub bottom and sides of fondue pot with garlic. Add champagne and place over medium heat until wine starts to bubble but not boil. Add cheese, a handful at a time, stirring constantly until cheese is melted before adding more. After all cheese is melted, bring the mixture to a boil. Remove from heat; add cognac, salt, and paprika. Transfer to fondue stand over low flame. Now the fun begins. Each person dips bread into the cheese mixture, swirling with a figure-eight motion, then eats and enjoys the good food. It is traditional that kirsch be sipped along with the meal. 4 to 6 servings.

MENU
Champagne Fondue
Endive and Orange Salad
Cherries Jubilee
Demitasse   Kirsch

Classic Swiss Fontina

½ to 1 teaspoon caraway seeds
¼ teaspoon celery seeds (optional)
1 pound Gruyère or Emmenthaler cheese
2 loaves crusty French bread
2 tablespoons butter or margarine
3 tablespoons flour
2 to 2½ cups scalded milk
Salt or seasoned salt to taste
Dash nutmeg

Beforehand Preparation

Soak caraway and celery seeds in hot water for 15 minutes; strain. Mince, grate, or shred cheese. Cut bread in crusty 1-inch pieces.

Tabletop Technique

In fondue pot melt butter; add flour; stir over low flame until thoroughly blended. Slowly add milk, then caraway and celery seeds; bring to a boil and reduce heat to keep sauce gently bubbling. Add cheese, one handful at a time, stirring until cheese melts; repeat. Add salt and nutmeg. Add hot milk as needed. Now the fun begins. Each Fontina fan spears a bread cube through the soft part out to the crusty side and dunks the tidbit into the fondue, swirls it around and repeats until his appetite is satisfied. 4 servings.

MENU
Classic Swiss Fontina
Marinated Tomato Chunks on Shredded Lettuce
Fresh Peaches with Raspberry Jam Sauce
Sugar Cookies   Spiced Tea

French Fried Camembert with Apple Slices

6 (1¾-ounce) wedges Camembert cheese
4 to 6 delicious apples
2 eggs, slightly beaten
1 cup fine dry bread crumbs
1½ cups peanut oil

Beforehand Preparation

Chill cheese and apples. Cut each cheese wedge
into 3 or 4 chunks. Dip in beaten eggs and bread
crumbs.

Tabletop Technique

At range in fondue pot, heat oil to boiling. Transfer to fondue stand over medium heat. Keep oil
bubbling hot. Spear cheese chunks on fondue
forks and cook in hot oil for about ½ minute.
Serve each person an apple and a fruit knife to
peel and cut the apple into thin crisp slices to eat
with hot cheese. 4 to 6 servings.

MIDNIGHT SNACK MENU
French Fried Camembert with Apple Slices
Crackers
Beer

Gruyère Fondue

1 loaf unsliced whole wheat bread
3 cups shredded Gruyère cheese
2 tablespoons potato flour
1 clove garlic
1¼ cups dry white wine
3 tablespoons brandy
¼ teaspoon prepared mustard
Dash pepper
Dash nutmeg

Beforehand Preparation
Cut bread into bite-size cubes. Toast in 325°F. oven for 15 minutes, turning every 5 minutes. Shred cheese and toss with flour.

Tabletop Technique
Rub fondue pot with cut clove of garlic. At range pour wine into fondue pot and warm over a medium flame until bubbles start to rise; do not boil. Toss in cheese, a handful at a time until all cheese has been smoothly blended in. When mixture begins to bubble, stir in brandy and seasonings. Transfer to fondue stand over medium heat. Spear bread cubes on fondue forks. Swirl in figure-eight motion in sauce. If fondue becomes too thick, add a little more warmed wine until of proper consistency. 4 servings.

MENU
Gruyère Fondue
Belgian Endive and Marinated Tomato Salad
Strawberry and Rhubarb Pie
Coffee   Brandy

Italian-Swiss Fondue

1 pound aged Swiss cheese
¼ cup tomato juice
2 tablespoons cornstarch
½ teaspoon salt
½ teaspoon Worcestershire sauce
½ teaspoon crushed basil leaves
¼ teaspoon pepper
¼ teaspoon nutmeg
1 or 2 loaves Italian wheat bread
1¾ cups tomato juice
1 clove garlic

Beforehand Preparation

Grate or chop cheese into mealy pieces. Combine ¼ cup tomato juice, cornstarch, salt, Worcestershire sauce, basil, pepper, and nutmeg. Cut bread into bite-size pieces with crust on one side.

Tabletop Technique

In fondue pot heat remaining tomato juice with garlic clove until almost boiling. Remove garlic, add cheese, a small amount at a time, stirring constantly until cheese is melted; it will be rather mealy at this point. Add cornstarch-seasoning mixture, stirring until smooth. Spear pieces of bread and stir in fondue with a figure-eight motion. Add more warm tomato juice if sauce becomes too thick. 6 servings.

MENU
Italian-Swiss Fondue
Broccoli Salad with Italian Dressing
Strawberries in White Wine
Caffè Espresso   White Wine

Tippler's Cheese Fondue

1 pound Swiss cheese
3 tablespoons flour
2 loaves crusty French bread
1 clove garlic
2 cups dry white wine
1½ ounces dark rum
1½ ounces brandy
1½ ounces kirsch
½ teaspoon salt
Dash each pepper and nutmeg

Beforehand Preparation

Shred cheese; lightly mix with flour. Cut bread into bite-size pieces with crust on one side.

Tabletop Technique

Rub fondue pot with garlic. Pour in wine; heat almost to boiling. Add large spoonfuls of cheese, stirring with wooden spoon until each lot is melted before adding more. When mixture is smooth, adjust heat to maintain gentle bubbling. Add rum, brandy, and kirsch. Season with salt, pepper, and nutmeg. Add warm wine if mixture becomes too thick. Spear bread on fondue fork, securing points of fork into crust. Dunk with stirring motion. 4 to 6 servings.

MENU
Tippler's Cheese Fondue
Apple Nut Salad
Petit Fours
Coffee   Dry White Wine

Traditional Swiss Cheese Fondue

1 pound aged Swiss cheese, Emmenthaler or
   Gruyère
3 tablespoons flour
2 loaves crusty French bread
1 plump clove fresh garlic
2 cups Neuchâtel or other dry white wine
1 tablespoon lemon juice
3 tablespoons kirsch
Dash each nutmeg and paprika

Beforehand Preparation

Mince, grate, or shred cheese; toss with flour. Cut
bread into 1-inch cubes with a crust on one side.
Peel garlic clove.

Tabletop Technique

Rub fondue pot with garlic clove; discard garlic.
Pour wine into pot. Set over moderate heat; bring
to a simmer, but do not boil. Add lemon juice.
Add a handful of cheese, stirring with wooden
spoon until melted; repeat until all cheese is used.
Heat to simmering. Add kirsch and spices; stir
until blended. Adjust burner so fondue will simmer slowly. Each guest spears on fondue fork
a cube of bread through soft side to crust to keep
it from slipping. Bread is dunked and swirled in
cheese. If fondue thickens, add a little hot wine.
4 servings.

MENU
Traditional Swiss Cheese Fondue
Tossed Green Salad
Ambrosia
White Wine   Coffee   Kirsch

Welsh Rabbit Fondue

1 pound aged Cheddar cheese
1 (12-ounce) can beer
1½ teaspoons dry mustard
1 teaspoon Worcestershire sauce
⅛ teaspoon celery salt
⅛ teaspoon white pepper
1 teaspoon paprika
1 large loaf, whole wheat or French bread
1 tablespoon butter

Beforehand Preparation

Shred cheese. Open beer and let stand at room temperature several hours before using. Combine mustard, Worcestershire sauce, celery salt, pepper, and paprika. Cut bread into 1-inch cubes with crust on one side, toast lightly if desired.

Tabletop Technique

At range in fondue pot, melt butter. Add cheese, ⅓ cup at a time; as cheese melts, gradually add 1 cup beer, stirring constantly with wooden spoon. Add blended seasonings. Transfer to fondue stand over low heat; keep cheese mixture at a slow simmer, just bubbling. Spear bread cubes through soft side to the crust to keep from slipping. Dunk into cheese and swirl at bottom of pot in a figure-eight motion to stir up sauce at bottom of pot. 4 to 6 servings.

MENU
Welsh Rabbit Fondue
Apple, Pecan and Orange Salad
with Fruit Salad Dressing
Toasted Pound Cake   Coffee   Beer

7

Meat
Poultry
Fish
and Other Fondues

The tempuras of Japan, the Fritto Mistos of Italy, and the famous deep-fried food of our own southland are reflected in this chapter. But, weight-watchers read on! There's good news for you. If food is quickly cooked in hot oil and drained on a napkin, the nutrition is locked in while little of the fat remains. An even more slenderizing idea is to substitute canned chicken or beef broth or consommé as the cooking liquid.

Trim meat of all fat before cutting into bite-size pieces or thin squares. To sliver meat, that is, to cut it into thin squares, partially freeze for easier slicing.

Fill the pot about ⅓ full with oil. If pot contains too much oil, it will splatter. If the oil starts to smoke, remove it from the fire until it cools somewhat and smoking has stopped for a few minutes. The classic fondue pot with sloping sides is designed to keep the hot oil from spattering.

Arrange pieces of raw meat, chicken, or fish on a lettuce or leaf-padded platter for an eye-appealing and therefore appetizing effect.

Alaskan King Crab Fondue

2 (6-ounce) packages frozen Alaska King Crab
2 (10-ounce) packages frozen French fried potatoes
1 lemon
1 tablespoon finely chopped parsley
1 clove garlic
1½ cups peanut oil
½ cup butter

Beforehand Preparation
Thaw and dry crab and potatoes; cut crab into bite-size pieces. Keep crab and potatoes refrigerated until serving time. Slice lemon into thin slices; coat in chopped parsley.

Tabletop Technique
Rub fondue pot with garlic clove. At range heat oil and butter to bubbling. Transfer to fondue stand over medium flame; keep bubbling hot. On fondue fork spear a piece of crab; immerse in hot oil-butter until cooked through, about ¾ of a minute. Then cook potato pieces, one or two at a time, until heated through. Repeat and enjoy. 4 servings.

MENU
Alaskan King Crab Fondue
Wilted Cucumber and Onion Salad
Chocolate Nut Brownies
Rum Coffee   White Wine

Barbados Chicken Fondue

4 chicken breasts
Chutney Sauce*
Toasted grated coconut
1 cup peanut oil
½ cup butter
½ teaspoon crushed red pepper
¼ teaspoon ginger
4 bananas

Beforehand Preparation

Buy boned chicken breasts to save time if you're in a hurry. Cut chicken into skinless strips or thin squares. Prepare Peach Chutney Sauce and coconut.

Tabletop Technique

At range in fondue pot, heat oil and butter to bubbling. Transfer to fondue stand over medium flame. Add red pepper and ginger. Keep oil at a constant bubble. Each person is served a portion of chicken and a banana to peel and cut into slices; pieces of each are alternately speared and immersed into hot oil until cooked to a light brown, about 1 minute, then dipped in Peach Chutney Sauce or coconut. Serves 4.

MENU
Barbados Chicken Fondue
Green Bean Vinaigrette Salad
Pineapple Sherbet with Crême de Menthe
Mocha Coffee   White Wine

*Instructions for preparing the sauces marked with an asterisk may be found by consulting the Index.

Beef Bourguignonne Fondue

2 pounds beef tenderloin or sirloin, well
   trimmed
Béarnaise Sauce*
Horseradish Sauce*
Spicy Tomato Sauce*
Anchovy Mustard Sauce*
1 clove garlic
1 cup (2 sticks) butter
1 cup salad oil

Beforehand Preparation

Cut beef into ¾-inch cubes. Prepare sauces.

Tabletop Technique

Rub fondue pot with garlic. Place pot on a roomy
platter or tray. Over low to medium heat melt
butter; add oil and heat thoroughly; keep hot but
not foaming. Serve beef cubes and sauces to each
guest. Everyone spears a piece of beef and cooks
it in the hot butter mixture until done to taste—
about 1 minute for rare; 1½ minutes for medium;
and 2 minutes for well done. Use a second fork to
dip meat into sauces and eat. 4 to 6 servings.

MENU

Beef Bourguignonne Fondue
Sauces
French Fried Potatoes
Mixed Greens, Red Onion, and Avocado Salad
Lime Sherbet with Chocolate Sauce
Demitasse   Burgundy

Beef Steak and Kidney Fondue

1 pound lean, boneless beef sirloin
8 lamb kidneys
½ pound mushrooms
Brown Sauce*
1 clove garlic
1½ cups peanut oil

Beforehand Preparation

Remove tissues and fat from beef; cut into 1-inch cubes. Remove core and tissues from lamb kidneys; cut into ¾-inch cubes. Wash and stem mushrooms; cut into ¼-inch slices. Prepare sauce.

Tabletop Technique

Rub fondue pot with garlic clove. At range heat oil to bubbling. Transfer to fondue stand over medium heat; keep oil bubbling hot but not foaming. Alternately cook cubes of beef, cubes of kidney, and slices of mushrooms in hot oil, cooking until done to taste. Dunk in Brown Sauce with dinner fork. Serves 4 to 6.

MENU
Beef Steak and Kidney Fondue
Brown Sauce
Toasted Buttered Hard Rolls
Potato Salad Garnished with Crisp Bacon Bits
Crushed Strawberries over Strawberry Ice Cream
Irish Coffee   Red Wine

Breakfast Party Fondue

1 egg, beaten
1 cup light cream or milk
3 tablespoons sugar
¼ teaspoon salt
4 slices sandwich bread
1 cup graham cracker crumbs
1 (8-ounce) package precooked pork sausage
1 (13¼-ounce) can pineapple chunks
Teriyaki Sauce*
Chutney Sauce*
2 cups salad oil

Beforehand Preparation

Mix together egg, cream, sugar, and salt. Dip bread slices into mixture, then coat with cracker crumbs. Cut into 1-inch squares. Chill for 1 hour. Cut sausages into 1-inch chunks. Drain pineapple (reserve juice for future use). Prepare sauces.

Tabletop Technique

In fondue pot heat oil to boiling but not smoking. Using fondue forks or long wooden skewers, alternately spear chunks of bread, sausage, and pineapple and dunk into hot fat and cook until browned. Dip into sauces. 4 servings.

MENU
Frosted "V-8" Juice
Breakfast Party Fondue
Coffee

Budget Beef Fondue

2 pounds round steak
1 teaspoon meat tenderizer
Herb Sauce*
Dill Sauce*
Chutney Sauce*
1 clove garlic
2 cups peanut oil

Beforehand Preparation

Trim fat and tissues from steak. Cut into 1-inch cubes. Sprinkle with a little water to moisten and then with meat tenderizer. Let stand for 1 hour. Dry meat (wet or cold meat will splatter). Prepare sauces.

Tabletop Technique

Rub fondue pot with garlic. Place on a roomy platter or tray. In pot heat oil to bubbling or until a small piece of bread browns in 1 minute. If oil begins to smoke, remove from burner immediately. Serve each guest meat cubes and a variety of sauces. They then spear meat and cook in oil (about 1 minute for rare, 1½ minutes for medium, and 2 minutes for well done) and dip the pieces in the sauces. 4 to 6 servings.

MENU
Budget Beef Fondue
Sauces
Herbed French Bread
Mixed Green Salad
Banana Cream Pie
Coffee   Beer

Cheese, Shrimp, and Rye Fondue

½ pound Swiss cheese
1 tablespoon flour
1 loaf unsliced rye bread
2 (10-ounce) cans frozen condensed cream of
    shrimp soup
1 clove garlic
¼ cup dry white wine

Beforehand Preparation

Shred or finely chop cheese; toss with flour. Cut bread into crusty chunks. Thaw soup. Peel and cut garlic clove.

Tabletop Technique

At range rub fondue pot with garlic. Pour in soup and wine. Add cheese, a handful at a time, stirring constantly over medium heat until cheese is completely melted. Transfer to fondue stand over low flame. To serve, spear bread chunks through to crust on fondue forks or long wooden skewers and dip into fondue, swirling in figure-eight motion to coat bread and stir fondue at bottom of pot. 6 servings.

MENU

Cheese, Shrimp, and Rye Fondue
Lettuce and Hearts of Palm Salad
Strawberry, Banana, Orange Compote
Demitasse   White Wine

Columbia Salmon Fondue

1 pound fresh or frozen salmon steaks
1 quart shelled oysters
1 cup fine cracker crumbs
2 cucumbers
Caper Sauce*
Dill Sauce*
2 cups salad oil
Coarsely ground pepper

Beforehand Preparation

Cut salmon into thin 1-inch squares. Drain oysters; roll in cracker crumbs. Cut cucumbers into 1-inch chunks, discarding seeded center. Prepare sauces.

Tabletop Technique

In fondue pot heat oil to bubbling but not foaming. Spear pieces of salmon, cucumber, or an oyster on fondue fork. Cook in hot oil until done, about 1 minute for salmon, ¼ to ½ minute for oysters or cucumber. Dip in sauces. Sprinkle coarsely ground pepper over salmon. 4 to 6 servings.

MENU
Columbia Salmon Fondue
Noisette Potatoes
Grilled Tomato Halves
Pineapple Cheese Strudel
Coffee   Dry White Wine

Fillet of Sole in Clam Juice Fondue

1½ pounds fillet of sole
1 lemon
Tartar Sauce*
Dill Sauce*
Pink Paprika Sauce*
1 clove garlic
3 cups clam juice
½ to 1 teaspoon seasoned salt
Dash hot pepper sauce

Beforehand Preparation

Cut fish into 1-inch thin squares; sprinkle with lemon juice. Chill until cooking time, then pat dry. Prepare sauces.

Tabletop Technique

Rub fondue pot with clove of garlic. Add clam juice, seasoned salt, and hot pepper sauce; heat to rolling boil. Then the fun begins as each person spears a piece of fish on a fondue fork or wooden skewer, cooks it in simmering clam juice until fish turns white and is cooked through, about 1 to 2 minutes, and dips it into one of the sauces. Do not overcook fish pieces or they will break. Add heated clam juice as needed. 4 to 6 servings.

MENU
Frosted "V-8" Juice with Mint Sprig
Fillet of Sole in Clam Juice Fondue
Sauces
Cucumber and Chopped Anchovy Salad
Brownies à la Mode
Coffee   White Wine

Fiori di Zucchini Indorati
(Batter-Fried Zucchini and Blossoms)

3 eggs
1 cup sifted flour
1 teaspoon salt
Dash pepper
2 to 3 tablespoons water or milk
24 squash blossoms
1 pound tender young zucchini
2 cups peanut or salad oil
Pepper grinder

Beforehand Preparation

Beat eggs until lemon colored; add flour gradually, mixing constantly. Stir in salt, pepper, and enough water so batter flows from a spoon easily but firmly. Remove squash blossoms from stems. Cut zucchini into ¼-inch slices. Lightly dry blossoms and slices.

Tabletop Technique

Heat oil in fondue pot until bubbling but not smoking. Serve each person a saucer of batter and a portion of squash blossoms and zucchini. Guests spear the blossoms or slices, thoroughly coat them in batter, then cook them in hot fat until batter begins to brown. Season with a generous sprinkle of freshly ground pepper. 4 to 6 servings.

MENU
Antipasto
Fiori di Zucchini Indorati
Toasted Italian Rolls
Rice Pudding with Zabaglione
Caffè al Diavolo   *Red Wine*

Flemish Beef Fondue

¾ cup beer
1 onion, sliced
½ bay leaf
¼ teaspoon crushed rosemary
1 whole clove
¼ teaspoon pepper
½ teaspoon salt
1 teaspoon chopped parsley
1 pound lean, boneless round of beef
2 cups Cheddar cheese cubes
Béarnaise Sauce*
Whipped Cream Horseradish Sauce*
1 clove garlic
2 cups salad oil

Beforehand Preparation

In saucepan combine beer, onion, bay leaf, rosemary, clove, pepper, salt, and parsley; heat to just boiling; remove from heat. Cut beef into 1-inch cubes. Pour hot marinade over beef. Cover; chill for several hours or overnight. Remove beef; pat dry. Prepare cheese cubes and sauces.

Tabletop Technique

At range rub fondue pot with garlic. Pour oil into pot and heat to a boil but not smoking. Transfer to fondue stand over medium flame. On fondue forks or skewers alternately spear cubes of meat and cheese cubes and cook in hot oil until cooked and browned. Dip into sauces. 4 servings.

MENU
Flemish Beef Fondue
Chilled Broccoli Vinaigrette
Chocolate Log   Demitasse   Red Wine

Freezer Seafood Fondue

1 (9-ounce) package frozen fish sticks
1 (8-ounce) package frozen fried clams
1 (7-ounce) package frozen miniature deviled
    crab
1 (7-ounce) package frozen breaded scallops
1 (6-ounce) package frozen fried shrimp
Tartar Sauce*
1 clove garlic
2 cups peanut oil
1½ cups seafood cocktail sauce

Beforehand Preparation
At room temperature thoroughly defrost and dry
all frozen foods. Cut fish sticks into 1-inch chunks.
Prepare Tartar Sauce.

Tabletop Technique
Rub fondue pot with garlic. In fondue pot at
range, heat oil to bubbling. Transfer to fondue
stand over medium flame; keep oil bubbling. Each
person spears a seafood tidbit on fondue fork,
cooks it in oil for about 1 minute, until golden
brown, then dips the piece into one of the sauces.
About 10 to 12 servings.

MENU
Freezer Seafood Fondue
Apple Cabbage Slaw
Garlic French Bread
Rainbow Ice Cream with Rainbow Sprinkles
Mocha Coffee   White Wine

French Dip Fondue

2 pounds roast beef
2 (10½-ounce) cans condensed consommé
1 teaspoon Worcestershire sauce
Dash garlic salt
2 teaspoons prepared mustard or horseradish
6 French or submarine rolls

Beforehand Preparation
Slice about 24 slices of roast beef. Combine consommé, Worcestershire sauce, garlic salt, and mustard. Stir to blend. Split rolls in half, then each into 3 double chunks.

Tabletop Technique
Pour consommé mixture into fondue pot. Heat to simmering. On fondue forks heat beef slices in consommé; remove and place on bottom halves of roll slices. Dip top sides of chunks, cut-side down, into consommé and use to close sandwiches. Eat while hot. 6 servings.

MENU
French Dip Fondue
Mixed Green Salad with Green Goddess Dressing
Cherry Tarts à la Mode
Demitasse   Burgundy

Fritto Misto

1 cup cauliflowerettes
1 cup cut Italian green beans
1 cup cooked chicken, veal, or pork
1 cup cooked, shelled, and deveined shrimp
1 cup firm cheese, Mozzarella or Bel Paese
1 (6- or 7-ounce) can artichoke hearts
1½ cups fine seasoned bread crumbs
4 eggs
Italian Sauce*
2 lemons
Parsley
1 clove garlic
2 cups salad oil

Beforehand Preparation

The foods may be leftovers and therefore need no extra cooking. If food is uncooked, cook to just done state; do not overcook. Cook cauliflowerettes and green beans until just crisp. Cook meat and shrimp; cut into bite-size pieces. Cut cheese into ¾-inch cubes. Thoroughly drain artichoke hearts. Roll all pieces in bread crumbs; let stand until dry. Beat eggs with ¼ cup water or milk. Dip all pieces in egg; roll again in crumbs; let stand until dry. Prepare sauce.

Tabletop Technique

Rub fondue pot with garlic. Heat oil to bubbling but not smoking. Spear one or more tidbits and cook in hot fat. Eat with a squeeze of lemon juice or a dip in the sauce.

MENU
Fritto Misto   Italian Wheat Bread
Pistachio Ice   Caffè Espresso   Vin del Paese

Frittura Fondue

1 small eggplant
6 ribs celery
3 small firm tomatoes
2 dozen frying clams
1½ cups seasoned, fine bread crumbs
3 eggs
1 lemon
Herb Sauce*
Watercress
1 clove garlic
2 cups salad oil

Beforehand Preparation

Peel eggplant; cut into 1-inch cubes. Cut celery into 1-inch pieces. Parboil eggplant and celery for 4 minutes. Cut tomatoes into thick slices and each slice into quarters. Drain clams; remove gritty neck collars; drain. Roll vegetable pieces and clams in bread crumbs; let stand until dry. Beat eggs with 2 to 3 tablespoons water. Dip all pieces into egg; roll again in bread crumbs; let stand until dry. Slice lemon thin. Prepare sauce.

Tabletop Technique

Rub fondue pot with garlic. Heat oil to bubbling but not smoking. On forks or skewers spear one or more tidbits and cook in hot fat. Eat with a squeeze of lemon or a dip in the sauce. 4 to 6 servings.

MENU
Frittura Fondue   Bread Sticks
Mixed Lettuce Salad with Anchovy Dressing
Chilled Spiced Pears with Hot Zabaglione Sauce
Filtered Coffee   White Chianti

El Gran Frou Frou
(A Spanish Beef and Mushroom Fondue)

1½ pounds tender lean boneless beef
½ pound mushrooms
1 large green pepper
1 clove garlic
Horseradish Sauce*
Spicy Tomato Sauce*
½ cup olive oil
1 cup peanut oil

Beforehand Preparation
Trim and cube beef into 1-inch squares. Wash and cut mushrooms into ¼-inch thick slices. Cut green pepper into 1-inch squares. Mash garlic through garlic press. Prepare sauces.

Tabletop Technique
At range heat oils and garlic to sizzling. Transfer to fondue stand over medium flame; keep bubbling but not foaming. Spear a slice of mushroom or green pepper with a beef cube on wooden skewers; cook in hot oil for ¾ (rare) to 2 (well done) minutes until done to taste. Use a dinner fork to dip meat and vegetables into sauces. Makes 4 servings.

MENU
El Gran Frou Frou
Horseradish Sauce
Spicy Tomato Sauce
Hot Fluffy Rice
Tomato, Stuffed Olive, and Caper Salad
Vanilla Flan
Demitasse   Sangría

Gulf Coast Shrimp and Avocado Fondue

2 cups shredded Swiss cheese
1 large red sweet onion
3 navel oranges
1 large avocado
1 tablespoon lemon juice
1 loaf French bread
1 (10-ounce) can frozen condensed cream of
    shrimp soup
1 cup milk
1 tablespoon dry sherry

Beforehand Preparation

Shred cheese. Slice and separate onion into rings.
Peel and section oranges; cut segments in half.
Just before serving, peel and cut avocado into
1-inch pieces; brush with lemon juice. Cut bread
into bite-size pieces with crust on one side. Thaw
soup.

Tabletop Technique

In fondue pot combine soup and milk; heat until
simmering. Add cheese, a handful at a time,
stirring after each addition until cheese is melted
and mixture is thoroughly blended. Stir in sherry.
Spear a ring of onion, a chunk of orange, bread,
or avocado and cook in gently bubbling soup for
about ½ minute or so. 4 servings.

MENU
Gulf Coast Shrimp and Avocado Fondue
Raisin and Carrot Cole Slaw
Chocolate Chiffon Pie
Demitasse   Beer

Honolulu Fondue

2 large whole chicken breasts, slightly frozen
½ pound cooked ham, 1-inch thick
2 cups pineapple cubes
½ cup pineapple juice
½ cup orange juice
1 cup dry white wine
1 tablespoon cornstarch
1 teaspoon grated orange rind
2 teaspoons brown sugar
1 teaspoon curry powder
Dash salt

Beforehand Preparation

Slice chicken breasts into thin 1-inch squares. Cut ham into 1-inch cubes. Drain pineapple, reserving liquid. Combine ½ cup pineapple juice, orange juice, and wine. Stir cornstarch smooth with ¼ cup of juice-wine liquid. Grate orange rind.

Tabletop Technique

In fondue pot heat wine-juice combination to almost boiling. Add cornstarch mixture, stirring with wooden spoon until smooth and slightly thickened. Add orange rind, brown sugar, curry powder, and salt; stir until thoroughly blended. Spear pieces of chicken, ham, or pineapple; dip into mixture and cook until done or heated through. 4 to 6 servings.

MENU
Honolulu Fondue
Saffron Rice   Cheese and Crackers
Tea   Dry White Wine or Sake

"Lemon" Sole Fondue

1 pound fillet of sole or other tender white fish
¼ cup lemon juice
1 teaspoon grated onion
Anchovy Mustard Sauce*
Caper Sauce*
1 clove garlic
2 cups dry white wine
¼ teaspoon dried dill weed

Beforehand Preparation

Cut fish into 1-inch squares; place in bowl; cover with lemon juice and marinate for 1 hour; remove and pat dry. Grate onion. Prepare sauces.

Tabletop Technique

Rub fondue pot with garlic clove. Heat wine almost to boiling. Add onion and dill weed. Spear fish pieces with fondue fork and cook in hot wine for about 1 minute or until done. Dip cooked pieces into sauces. 4 servings.

MENU
"Lemon" Sole Fondue
French Fried Potatoes
Spinach Soufflé
Strawberries Flambé
Demitasse   Dry White Wine

Marinated Chicken Fondue

1 (6-ounce) can frozen pineapple-orange juice
    concentrate
2 tablespoons salad oil
1 teaspoon ginger
1 teaspoon soy sauce
4 chicken breasts (about 1½ pounds)
Teriyaki Sauce*
Grated coconut
Peanuts, chopped fine
1 clove garlic
2 cups salad oil

Beforehand Preparation

Combine undiluted juice, oil, ginger, and soy
sauce; bring to a boil; remove from heat. Remove
skin and bones from chicken breasts; cut into thin
1-inch squares. Pour hot marinade over chicken.
Cover and chill several hours or overnight. Remove chicken and pat dry. Save marinade for future use to baste chicken or ham. Prepare sauce,
coconut, and peanuts.

Tabletop Technique

Rub fondue pot with garlic. Heat oil to boiling
but not smoking. Spear chicken squares on fondue forks or long wooden skewers and cook in hot
oil until cooked to taste. Dip into sauce and then
into grated coconut or chopped nuts. 4 servings.

MENU
Marinated Chicken Fondue
Rice Pilaf
Hearts of Palm Salad
Cheesecake   *Espresso*   *Dry White Wine*

Marseilles Shellfish Fondue

12 small clams, fresh, frozen, or canned
12 oysters, fresh or frozen
12 mussels, fresh or canned
12 snails, fresh or canned
Parsley Butter
Dill Sauce*
1 clove garlic
3 to 4 cups clam and oyster juices
¼ teaspoon celery salt
Dash pepper
Cocktail Sauce*

Beforehand Preparation

Save fresh clam and oyster liquid. Rinse shellfish through several waters. Check to see that all sand is removed. Canned or frozen shellfish should not need rinsing. Prepare sauces.

Tabletop Technique

Rub fondue pot with garlic clove. Pour in clam and oyster juices, celery salt, and pepper. Over medium heat, heat until simmering. Serve portions of shellfish and sauces to each person. Spear pieces of shellfish on fondue forks or wooden skewers; cook in simmering juice until each piece is cooked to taste, about 1 to 1½ minutes. Dip in sauces. In case juice cooks down, add hot water. 4 servings.

MENU
Marseilles Shellfish Fondue
Sauce   Bibb Lettuce Salad
Lime Sherbet with Coconut
Demitasse   White Wine

Mini-Meatball Fondue

1 pound ground round steak
2 eggs, beaten
¼ cup evaporated milk
⅓ cup fine cracker crumbs
1 teaspoon salt
¼ teaspoon pepper
2 tablespoons grated onion
Pink Paprika Sauce*
Horseradish Sauce*
Tomato Relish Sauce*
1 clove garlic
2 cups salad oil

Beforehand Preparation

Combine all ingredients except sauces, garlic, and oil; shape into walnut-size meatballs; chill 1 hour. Prepare sauces.

Tabletop Technique

Rub fondue pot with garlic. Heat oil to boiling but not smoking. On fondue forks or long wooden skewers spear meatballs and cook in hot fat until crusty brown on the outside, about 1 to 2 minutes. Dip in sauces and enjoy. 4 to 6 servings.

MENU
Mini-Meatball Fondue
Barbecued Potato Chips
Mixed Vegetable Salad
Doughnut Ice Cream Sandwiches
Soft Drinks

Mixed Grill Fondue

1 pound chicken breasts, slightly frozen
1 pound fillet mignon, slightly frozen
½ pound lamb kidneys
2 green peppers
¼ pound bacon
Whipped Cream Horseradish Sauce*
Teriyaki Sauce*
Spicy Red Sauce*
1 clove garlic
1 cup salad oil
1 cup butter

Beforehand Preparation

Bone and skin chicken; slice chicken and beef into thin 1-inch squares. Remove fat and tubes from kidneys; slice into thin slices. Clean and remove seeds from green peppers. Cut into 1-inch squares. Cook bacon until crisp; drain and crumble. Prepare sauces.

Tabletop Technique

Rub fondue pot with clove of garlic. Heat oil and butter over medium flame to bubbling but not foaming. To serve, spear a piece of chicken, beef, kidney, or green pepper, and cook to taste for about 1 minute in hot fat. Dip in sauces, then in crumbled bacon. 4 to 6 servings.

MENU
Mixed Grill Fondue
Herbed French Bread
Chinese Cabbage Salad
Strawberry Ice Cream Pie
Demitasse   Rosé Wine

Oriental Fondue

½ to 1 pound lean flank steak, slightly frozen
½ pound chicken breasts, slightly frozen
½ pound shrimp
½ pound bulk lean ham
½ pound fresh mushrooms
½ pound fresh spinach leaves
½ pound Chinese cabbage
Kabuki Sauce*
Spicy Red Sauce*
Curry Sauce*
1 clove garlic
2 (10½-ounce) cans condensed chicken broth
1 (10½-ounce) can condensed beef broth

Beforehand Preparation

Slice steak into paper-thin 1-inch squares. Bone and skin chicken; slice into thin 1-inch squares. Peel and devein shrimp, leaving tails on. Cut ham into ¾-inch cubes. Clean mushrooms, spinach, and Chinese cabbage; cut into bite-size pieces; chill to keep crisp. Prepare sauces. Peel garlic.

Tabletop Technique

Rub fondue pot with garlic; discard garlic. Pour in chicken and beef broth. Set over high heat; bring to a boil. Reduce to medium heat but keep at a rolling boil. Using fork or skewer, each guest dips a piece of food into the broth, cooks the food for about 1 minute or less, then dips it in one of the sauces. 4 to 6 servings.

MENU

Oriental Fondue   Hot Fluffy Rice
Sauces   Toasted French Bread
Preserved Kumquats   Tea   Sake

Pacific Halibut Fondue

2 to 3 large potatoes
1½ pounds halibut steak
2 to 3 small zucchini
Spicy Red Sauce*
Teriyaki Sauce*
Tartar Sauce*
½ bunch parsley
1 large lemon or 2 limes
1 clove garlic
1 cup peanut or salad oil
½ cup butter or margarine

Beforehand Preparation

Dice potatoes into 1-inch cubes; parboil over medium heat until just tender, about 10 minutes; drain. Slice halibut steak into thin 1-inch squares. Cut zucchini into 1-inch cubes. Prepare sauces. Wash parsley and shake dry.

Tabletop Technique

Rub fondue pot with garlic. Heat oil and butter until bubbling. Each person alternately spears and dips pieces of halibut, zucchini, and potato into the hot mixture until delicately brown, about 1 minute. Squeeze lemon over. Dip the pieces into sauces on sectional dishes. You'll also enjoy spearing sprigs of parsley and cooking them in the oil—delicious, and a new idea. 4 to 6 servings.

MENU
Pacific Halibut Fondue
Sauces   *Mixed Green Salad*
Strawberries with Whipped Cream
Coffee with Cognac

Persian Lamb Fondue

2 pounds boneless lean lamb, cut from leg
1 cup Italian salad dressing
2 green peppers
6 outside stalks celery
1 pint cherry tomatoes
Spicy Red Sauce*
Curry Sauce*
Dill Sauce*
1 clove garlic
1 cup peanut oil
1 cup olive oil

Beforehand Preparation

Remove fat and tissues from lamb; cut into ¾-inch cubes. Marinate in salad dressing overnight; drain and pat dry. Wash and cut green peppers and celery into 1-inch pieces. Wash and stem tomatoes. Prepare sauces.

Tabletop Technique

Rub fondue pot with garlic clove. Place on a roomy tray. Heat oils until bubbling but not smoking. Each person alternately spears a cube of lamb or a vegetable piece on heat-proof fondue fork and cooks it in hot oil until done to taste, dips the piece into one of the sauces, then repeats the action. 4 to 6 servings.

MENU
Persian Lamb Fondue
Buttered, Toasted Hard Rolls
Lettuce Wedge with Chiffonade Dressing
Honey Cakes
Turkish Coffee   Red Wine

Potatoes in the Butter Pot

1 pound new potatoes
1 medium onion
½ cup butter or margarine
½ cup cider vinegar
½ teaspoon salt
⅛ teaspoon pepper

Beforehand Preparation
Boil potatoes in jackets until just tender; do not overcook; keep hot. Mince onion very fine.

Tabletop Technique
In fondue pot over medium-high heat, cook butter, vinegar, onion; salt and pepper until onion is tender. Bring hot potatoes to the table covered. Each person spears a potato, peels it, and dips bite-size pieces into the hot vinegar-butter. 4 servings.

MENU
Potatoes in the Butter Pot
Ham and Swiss Cheese Roll-ups
Mixed Vegetable Salad
Tipsy Pudding
Café au Lait   Kirsch

Shrimp Pepper Pot

24 large fresh shrimp
2 green peppers
2 medium chili peppers, crushed
1 large clove garlic
Spicy Tomato Sauce*
Remoulade Sauce*
1½ cups peanut oil
½ cup olive oil

Beforehand Preparation

Shell and devein shrimp; refrigerate until serving time. Cut green peppers into 1-inch squares. Crush chili peppers. Peel garlic; mash in garlic press. Prepare sauces.

Tabletop Technique

In fondue pot at range, heat oils to sizzling, but not smoking. Add crushed chili peppers and garlic. Adjust heat to keep oil bubbling. Spear a square of green pepper and a shrimp on fondue fork or wooden skewer. Cook in hot oil until shrimp is cooked, about 1 to 2 minutes. 4 servings.

MENU

Bisque of Tomato Soup
Shrimp Pepper Pot
Sauces
Hot Fluffy Rice
Artichoke Heart and Caper Salad
Fruits in Brandy
Turkish Coffee

Shrimp Tempura

1 pound (about 24) raw shrimp in shell
1 cup unsifted flour
1 teaspoon baking powder
1 teaspoon salt
2 eggs
½ cup milk
1 teaspoon peanut oil
Kabuki Sauce*
1½ to 2 cups peanut oil

Beforehand Preparation

Peel shrimp and split butterfly fashion, leaving tails on; devein. In a large bowl blend flour, baking powder, and salt. Combine eggs, milk, and 1 teaspoon oil; add to dry ingredients. Beat with egg beater until smooth. Prepare sauce.

Tabletop Technique

At range in fondue pot, heat remaining oil to bubbling. Transfer to fondue stand over medium flame; keep bubbling hot. Each person is served a portion of shrimp, batter, and sauce, in a separate bowl. Using fondue fork, shrimp is dipped in batter, then in hot oil and cooked until batter is puffy and golden brown. Serve with hot Kabuki Sauce. 4 to 6 servings.

MENU

Small Cups Chicken Broth with Blossom Floating
Shrimp Tempura   Hot Rice
Spinach, Radish, and Bacon Salad
With Lemon, Oil, and Vinegar Dressing
Mandarin Oranges with Chopped Almonds
Tea   Sake

Superb Chicken Liver Fondue

1½ pound chicken livers
½ pound fresh mushroom caps
4 medium-size potatoes
1 tablespoon lemon juice
1½ pounds fresh asparagus
½ bunch parsley
Hollandaise Sauce*
1 cup oil
1 cup butter

Beforehand Preparation

Clean chicken livers; cut into ¾-inch chunks. Clean mushrooms; cut into ¼-inch slices. Peel and cut potatoes into ¼-inch slices; soak in water with lemon juice to keep from turning brown; dry before serving. Clean asparagus; partially cook; drain and cut into 1-inch pieces. Chop parsley. Prepare sauce.

Tabletop Technique

Heat oil and butter in fondue pot until bubbling but not foaming. Keep oil bubbling over medium heat. To serve, spear a piece of chicken liver, mushroom, potato, or asparagus. Cook in hot oil about 1 minute or until done to taste. Dip chicken livers and potatoes in parsley. Dip asparagus and mushrooms into sauce. 4 to 6 servings.

MENU
Superb Chicken Liver Fondue
Belgian Endive and Pimento Salad
Toasted Dinner Rolls
Vanilla Ice Cream with Maple Rum Sauce
Coffee   Dry White Wine

8

Sauces
Add to the Fun

Mix several simple sauces or go all out and cook up a storm of three of four. With fondue there is no question—the more sauces the merrier, and the more delectable.

Be imaginative. There are dozens of combinations that you might "invent" to make your sauce repertoire delightfully individual. And give thought to other accompaniments that compliment certain foods, such as readily available pickles, relishes, preserved fruits, and other specialties.

For the meat, fish, and poultry fondues, you'll want different flavors, perhaps a selection of tart, sweet, pungent, and mild sauces.

Anchovy Mustard Sauce

1 (2-ounce) can anchovies, drained and chopped
1 tablespoon chopped chives
1 tablespoon chopped parsley
1 medium clove garlic, minced
⅓ cup cooking oil
3 tablespoons hot French mustard
2 tablespoons cider vinegar

Combine all ingredients and chill. Makes about ⅔ cup.

Béarnaise Sauce

2 egg yolks
1 tablespoon water
1 tablespoon tarragon vinegar
2 tablespoons cream
½ teaspoon salt
Dash hot pepper sauce
4 tablespoons butter
1 teaspoon chopped chives
1 teaspoon chopped fresh tarragon
1 teaspoon chopped fresh parsley

In earthenware bowl mix egg yolks, water, vinegar, cream, salt, and hot pepper sauce. Place bowl over saucepan of hot water over slow fire; stir with whisk until mixture begins to thicken. Add butter, bit by bit; whisk in chives, tarragon, and parsley, beating until thick and thoroughly blended. Serve hot. Makes ¾ cup.

Bechamel Sauce

2 tablespoons butter
2 tablespoons flour
1 tablespoon finely chopped onion
1 cup condensed chicken broth
½ teaspoon salt
⅛ teaspoon white pepper
2 tablespoons heavy cream

Melt butter; add flour, stirring smooth. Stir in onion. Gradually add chicken broth, stirring until smooth and thickened. Blend in seasonings and cream. Simmer over very low heat for 10 minutes. Strain. Makes about 1 cup.

Brown Sauce

2 tablespoons butter
½ cup minced ham
2 tablespoons chopped onion
1 small bay leaf
1 tablespoon flour
1 tablespoon tomato puree
1 cup condensed beef broth
Salt and pepper

Melt butter. Brown ham, onion, and bay leaf until onion is tender. Blend in flour and tomato puree; gradually add broth, stirring constantly. Simmer over low heat until thickened. Season to taste with salt and pepper. Strain. Makes about 1½ cups.

Caper Sauce

1 cup mayonnaise
¼ cup drained pickle relish
1 tablespoon drained capers, chopped
1½ teaspoons chopped parsley

Combine all ingredients; stir to blend. Chill for 1 hour before serving. Makes 1¼ cups.

Chutney Sauce

½ cup chutney
½ cup sugar
2 tablespoons lemon juice

Combine all ingredients in small saucepan. Simmer over low heat until syrupy. Makes ¾ cup.

Cucumber Mayonnaise

1 cup mayonnaise
½ cup finely chopped cucumber
1 teaspoon grated onion
½ teaspoon seasoned salt
Dash cayenne

Combine all ingredients. Chill for 2 hours or more.
Blend again before serving. Makes about 1½ cups.

Curry Mayonnaise

1 cup mayonnaise
1 to 2 teaspoons curry powder
Dash garlic salt
2 teaspoons snipped chives *or* parsley

Combine all ingredients, adding curry to taste;
stir to blend. Chill. Makes 1 cup.

Curry Sauce

2 tablespoons margarine or butter
¼ cup chopped onion
1 small clove garlic, minced
1 teaspoon celery flakes
1 teaspoon curry powder
¾ cup chicken broth
½ cup applesauce
Generous dash mace
Generous dash salt

Melt margarine in saucepan. Add onion, garlic, celery flakes, and curry powder. Cook over low heat until onion is tender. Add remaining ingredients. Simmer over low heat 5 minutes. Makes about 1⅓ cups.

Dill Sauce

1 cup dairy sour cream
2 tablespoons horseradish
2 tablespoons minced green onion
1 teaspoon sugar
¼ teaspoon dried dill weed
Generous dash salt
Dash pepper

Combine all ingredients and chill. Makes 1 cup.

Garlic Mayonnaise

1 cup mayonnaise
2 cloves garlic, mashed
1 teaspoon lemon juice
1 tablespoon finely chopped parsley

Combine all ingredients. Chill for 2 hours or more. Blend again before serving. Makes 1 cup.

Herb Sauce

½ cup (1 stick) margarine or butter
2 tablespoons chopped parsley
1 tablespoon chopped chives
¼ teaspoon dry mustard
⅛ teaspoon onion salt
⅛ teaspoon thyme, crushed

In a small saucepan, combine margarine with remaining ingredients. Heat over low heat until margarine is melted and sauce is hot. Makes about ½ cup.

Hollandaise Sauce

3 egg yolks
¼ teaspoon salt
Dash cayenne
1 tablespoon lemon juice
½ cup butter
3 tablespoons hot water

In heavy bowl beat egg yolks with a wooden spoon until just smooth. Add salt, cayenne, and lemon juice. Melt butter; stir into egg-yolk mixture. Add hot water. Set bowl over (but not touching) hot but not boiling water. Stir until thick, about 4 to 5 minutes. Store in refrigerator; reheat over hot water before serving. Makes about 1¼ cups.

Horseradish Sauce

⅓ cup milk
1 (8-ounce) package cream cheese, softened
1½ tablespoons drained, prepared horseradish
1 tablespoon snipped chives

Gradually blend milk into cream cheese. Mix well with remaining ingredients. Makes 1⅓ cups.

Italian Sauce

½ cup olive oil
½ cup cider vinegar
2 tablespoons chopped, drained capers
¼ teaspoon crumbled oregano
½ teaspoon salt
1 teaspoon aromatic bitters

Place all ingredients in a covered jar; shake well.
Makes 1 cup.

Kabuki Sauce

½ cup chopped onion
1 large clove garlic, minced
2 tablespoons peanut oil
½ cup soy sauce
⅓ cup water
¼ cup dry red wine
2 tablespoons sugar
1 tablespoon cornstarch
¼ teaspoon ground ginger

In small saucepan cook onion and garlic in oil
until onion is tender. Add remaining ingredients.
Heat, stirring until thickened. Cook over low
heat for 5 minutes; stir occasionally. Serve hot
with shrimp, fish, or chicken fondue. Makes about
1½ cups.

Mustard Mayonnaise

¾ cup mayonnaise
⅓ cup hot mustard

Stir ingredients together. Makes about 1 cup.

Pink Paprika Sauce

Add ½ to 1 tablespoon (to taste) hot Hungarian paprika to Bechamel sauce.

Remoulade Sauce

3 hard-cooked egg yolks
¾ cup mayonnaise
1 tablespoon tarragon vinegar
½ teaspoon dry mustard
1 tablespoon chopped gherkins
1 teaspoon anchovy paste
2 tablespoons heavy cream
2 teaspoons chopped parsley
1½ teaspoons aromatic bitters

Put egg yolks through sieve. Combine mayonnaise and vinegar with egg yolks and mustard. Blend thoroughly. Add remaining ingredients. Blend thoroughly. Makes 1 cup.

Spanish Red Sauce

2 tablespoons olive oil
1 clove garlic, minced
½ cup chopped onion
¼ cup chopped green pepper
¾ cup beef broth
1 (6-ounce) can tomato sauce
¼ cup chopped black olives
½ teaspoon crumbled oregano
¼ teaspoon crumbled thyme
½ teaspoon salt
Dash cayenne pepper

Heat olive oil in skillet. Add garlic, onion, and green pepper; sauté until onion and pepper are tender. Add remaining ingredients and simmer about 20 minutes, stirring occasionally. Makes about 2 cups.

Spicy Red Sauce

1 cup spicy ketchup
2 tablespoons chopped parsley
2 tablespoons lemon juice
1 teaspoon aromatic bitters

Combine all ingredients; blend. Chill. Makes 1¼ cups.

Spicy Tomato Sauce

¾ cup spicy ketchup
2 teaspoons prepared horseradish
1 tablespoon lemon juice
¼ teaspoon dry mustard
⅛ teaspoon salt
Dash cayenne

Combine all ingredients. Refrigerate at least 1 hour to blend flavors. Makes about ¾ cup.

Tartar Sauce

¾ cup mayonnaise
1 teaspoon grated onion
1 tablespoon chopped parsley
1 tablespoon chopped sweet pickle
1 tablespoon chopped green olives

Combine all ingredients. Refrigerate at least 1 hour to blend flavors. Makes about 1 cup.

Teriyaki Sauce

½ cup soy sauce
¼ cup white wine
2 teaspoons sugar
¼ teaspoon garlic powder

Combine all ingredients. Makes about ¾ cup. (Refrigerate unused sauce; it lasts for several months.)

Tomato Relish Sauce

1 cup chili sauce
¼ cup pickle relish
¼ teaspoon hot pepper sauce

Stir ingredients together. Makes 1¼ cups.

Whipped Cream Horseradish Sauce

½ cup heavy cream
2 to 3 tablespoons grated horseradish
1 teaspoon prepared mustard
Dash hot pepper sauce
Salt
2 tablespoons mayonnaise

Beat cream stiff. Add horseradish, mustard, pepper sauce, and salt to taste. Fold in mayonnaise. Chill. Makes 1⅓ cups.

9

Bread
for Fondues

Those with the creative spark who have tried and lost in the fields of painting, writing, or music, can find solace in French bread dough. The dough is remarkably versatile and can be turned into a number of shapes. It is sure to bring appreciative "ahs" from the family as it is served warm from the oven.

To know it is to knead it.

Biscuit Fruit Bundles

1 (8-ounce) can refrigerated flaky baking pow
    der biscuits
Pitted dates
Maraschino cherries
Raisins
Walnut or pecan halves
2 cups salad oil
Powdered sugar

Cut each refrigerated biscuit into 4 pieces. Shape dough around fruit or nut. Fry in hot oil (360°F.) about 2 to 3 minutes or until golden brown. Dip in powdered sugar. Makes 40 bundles.

Bread Sticks

Prepare Crusty Hard Roll dough, adding 2 tablespoons butter (omit cornmeal). Let dough rise until double in bulk (1½ to 2 hours). Punch down; roll into rectangle about 8x12 inches. Cut in half, lengthwise, then into 16 strips. Roll each on unfloured board to make smooth, even sticks about 9 inches long. Arrange 1 inch apart on cookie sheet. Let rise until double in bulk. Bake in 425°F. oven for 5 minutes. Reduce oven heat to 350°F.; bake 15 minutes longer. Makes 32 bread sticks.

Crusty Hard Rolls

1 package dry yeast
1 cup lukewarm milk
2 tablespoons butter
1 tablespoon sugar
1 teaspoon salt
2½ to 3 cups bread flour
1 egg white
Cornmeal

Combine yeast and milk; let stand 5 minutes. Add butter, sugar, and salt. Add 1½ cups flour and egg white. Beat vigorously for 5 minutes, or 2 minutes at low speed with an electric mixer. Gradually add enough flour to make dough just firm enough to handle. Knead until dough is smooth and elastic, about 5 to 8 minutes. Place in greased bowl; cover with slightly damp cloth. Set in a warm place and let rise until doubled in bulk (about 1½ to 2 hours). Punch down; divide into 18 equal parts. To shape, flatten each piece into an oval 5x3 inches. Fold edge of dough toward you, sealing well. With both hands roll gently back and forth to taper ends. Arrange 2 inches apart on buttered pans sprinkled with cornmeal; brush with melted butter. Cover with cloth. Let rise until double in bulk (about 1 hour). Bake in 400°F. oven with pan of boiling water on shelf beneath rolls. Makes about 18 rolls.

English Muffins

1 package dry yeast
1 cup lukewarm water
1 teaspoon salt
2 teaspoons sugar
3 tablespoons shortening, softened
3 cups bread flour
Cornmeal

Combine yeast and water; let stand for 5 minutes. Stir in salt, sugar, and shortening. Add 2 cups flour. Beat well. Add remaining flour. Knead on lightly floured board until dough is smooth and elastic, about 5 minutes. Let rise until double in bulk. Punch down; place on board sprinkled with cornmeal. Roll to about ½-inch thickness. Cut with 3-inch biscuit cutter. Chill until ready to bake. Bake 15 minutes on hot buttered griddle, turning several times. To toast, use tines of fork to puncture all around edge of muffins. Gently pull apart, turning slowly. Butter and toast under broiler for best results. Makes 12 muffins.

French Bread

1 package active dry yeast
1¼ cups warm water (not hot—110° to 115°)
1½ teaspoons salt
3 tablespoons soft shortening
4 cups sifted all-purpose flour
cornmeal
1 egg white
2 tablespoons water

In mixing bowl dissolve yeast in water. Stir in salt and shortening and half the flour; mix with spoon. Add rest of flour; mix with hand. Turn onto lightly floured board. Knead until smooth and elastic. Round up in greased bowl; bring greased side up. Cover with damp cloth. Let rise in warm place (85°) until double in bulk, 1½ to 2 hours. Punch down; round up; let rise again until almost double in bulk, about 45 minutes. Punch down; cover; let rest 15 minutes. Roll into oblong, 15x 10 inches. Roll up tightly; seal edge. With both hands roll gently back and forth to taper ends. Place on lightly greased baking sheet (sprinkled lightly with cornmeal). Make ¼-inch slashes in dough at 2-inch intervals or 1 slash lengthwise. Brush top with cold water. Let stand uncovered about 1½ hours. Brush again. Heat oven to 375° F. Bake 20 minutes. Remove from oven and brush with mixture of egg white and 2 tablespoons water. Return to oven and bake 25 minutes longer.

French Rolls

To make rolls, divide French bread dough into 2½-ounce balls, about 18 in all. Flatten dough with the side of the hand and roll it up, tapering the ends. Make a slit about ¼-inch deep from end to end on each roll. Bake 20 to 25 minutes at 450° F. Brush on egg white/water glaze 10 minutes before baking is done.

Garlic Bread

Slice loaf of French bread diagonally; spread slices with garlic butter. Wrap loaf in aluminum foil and heat in a preheated 400°F. oven. You can use butter flavored with garlic salt or allow a cut of garlic to rest in ¼ cup butter for 30 minutes.

Parmesan Squares for Dipping

2 eggs
4 drops hot pepper sauce
2 tablespoons butter, melted
4 slices bread
6 ounces Parmesan cheese, grated

Beat eggs; add pepper sauce and butter; stir until well blended. Cut bread into 1-inch cubes. Dip cubes into egg mixture; roll in cheese. Chill for 1 hour. Spear and fry in hot oil until browned.

10

*Dip
into
Desserts*

A dessert fondue party is a happy roundtable occasion. The pot of sweet hot sauce, served at the dinner table or around a coffee table, is sure to be the focal point of lively conversation and convivial dipping.

The dunking foods might be cake, marshmallows, pieces of fruit, or a variety of dessert assortments. You have a choice of chocolate, liqueur, caramel sauces, and others described here in which to coat the sweets. The hot bon-bon pleasure of the dessert fondue pot surpasses the most exotic candy makers' skill.

Prepare sweet sauces in a double boiler or saucepan at the range—ahead of time if you like. Reheat at serving time and bring hot to the table, keeping sauces warm over low spirit or candle flame. Remember to brush fruits that darken with lemon juice after cutting.

Canned fruits are ideal if they are firm. Thoroughly drain them and arrange in an attractive display on green leaves. For an extra-special treat, have dishes of grated coconut, finely chopped nuts, or other finely chopped delicacies for a second dip after the sweet sauce coating.

Angel Fondue

4 cups strawberries
4 to 6 slices angel food cake
⅔ cup heavy cream
1 cup miniature marshmallows
2 tablespoons powdered sugar

Beforehand Preparation
Wash and hull strawberries. Cut angel cake into
1-inch cubes.

Tabletop Technique
In fondue pot over low heat, combine cream,
marshmallows, and sugar. Stir until blended and
marshmallows are melted. To serve, dip strawberries and cake alternately into hot sauce using
heat-proof fondue forks. 4 servings.

DESSERT MENU
Angel Fondue
Coffee   Brandy

Apricot Brandy Fondue

4 (1-inch) slices pound cake
1 cup chocolate syrup
2 cups miniature marshmallows
2 tablespoons apricot brandy
1 cup pitted dates
1 cup pecan halves
1 cup walnut halves

Beforehand Preparation
Toast cake slices; cut into 1-inch cubes.

Tabletop Technique
In fondue pot over heat, combine chocolate syrup, marshmallows, and brandy. Heat, stirring constantly until smooth. Serve a portion of cake, dates, and nuts to each guest to be swirled, one at a time, in hot chocolate sauce. 4 servings.

DESSERT MENU
Apricot Brandy Fondue
Iced Coffee with Rum

Apricot Ice Cream Sandwiches in Fudge Sauce

1 cup heavy cream
2 tablespoons sugar
1 tablespoon lemon juice
1 (7¾-ounce) jar apricot puree (baby food)
8 to 12 (¼-inch) slices pound cake
3 (3-ounce) bars sweet chocolate
2 tablespoons butter or margarine
⅔ cup heavy cream
2 tablespoons sugar

Beforehand Preparation

Whip cream; fold in sugar, lemon juice, and apricot puree. Arrange 4 to 6 slices pound cake in 8-inch square pan. Pour cream mixture over. Cover with remaining cake. Freeze until firm. Cut into 1-inch bite-size squares. Keep frozen until serving time. Break chocolate into small pieces.

Tabletop Technique

At range in fondue pot over water, melt chocolate; add butter, cream, and sugar. Stir with wooden spoon until well blended. Transfer to fondue stand over very low heat or candle flame. Spear frozen sandwiches and dip into gently bubbling chocolate fondue. 4 to 6 servings.

MENU
Apricot Ice Cream Sandwiches in Fudge Sauce
Hot Spiced Apple Cider

Banana Cheese Dessert Dunk

½ pound Emmenthaler or Gruyère cheese
2 tablespoons flour
1 cup dry white wine
¼ teaspoon nutmeg
Dash powdered clove
Salt to taste
4 to 6 bananas
1 to 1½ cups crushed cornflakes

Beforehand Preparation
Shred cheese; sift flour over cheese and toss.

Tabletop Technique
At range in fondue pot, heat wine to bubbling.
Add cheese, a handful at a time, stirring constantly with wooden fork or spoon until cheese
is melted and mixture bubbles. Add nutmeg, clove,
and salt to taste. Remove to fondue stand over
medium flame; keep cheese mixture at a constant
low bubble. Each person slices a banana into ½-
inch slices, dips slices into cheese, swirling until
heated through, then dunks slices into crumbs. 4
to 6 servings.

MENU
Banana Cheese Dessert Dunk
Coffee with Rum

Brandied, Candied Apple Wedges

4 large firm baking apples
2 tablespoons lemon juice
1 pint vanilla ice cream
Crushed peppermint candy
Chopped nuts
⅓ cup butter or margarine
1 cup brown sugar
¼ cup brandy
1 cup sweet apple cider
Dash ground cloves

Beforehand Preparation

Pare apples; cut in wedges; brush with lemon juice. Stir ice cream to soften; keep firm (not runny) in freezer. Crush peppermint candy; chop nuts.

Tabletop Technique

At range in fondue pot, heat butter, sugar, brandy, cider, and cloves to gentle boil, stirring with a wooden spoon. Transfer to fondue stand over low heat or candle. Serve softened ice cream, crushed candy, and chopped nuts to each guest. With fondue fork spear apple wedges. Dip into hot sauce and swirl in figure-eight motion until apples are coated, then in ice cream and candy or nuts. 4 servings.

MENU
Brandied, Candied Apple Wedges
Cappucino

Brandied Chocolate Fruit Fondue

1 (17-ounce) can fruits for salad
1 (11-ounce) can mandarin oranges
1 cup semi-sweet chocolate morsels
1 tablespoon water
2 tablespoons heavy cream
2 tablespoons brandy
1½ teaspoons instant coffee powder
Dash cinnamon

Beforehand Preparation
Drain fruit, saving juices for future use; cut into
bite-size pieces.

Tabletop Technique
In fondue pot over very low heat, combine chocolate and water; stir until chocolate melts and is
smooth. Add cream, brandy, coffee powder, and
cinnamon. Stir until smooth. Keep warm over
very low spirit or candle flame. To serve, dip
fruit pieces into sauce, using heat-proof fondue
forks. 4 to 6 servings.

MENU
Brandied Chocolate Fruit Fondue
Demitasse   Champale

Butterscotch Fondue

6 (1-inch) slices pound cake
2 ounces unsweetened chocolate
1 cup chopped pecans or walnuts
½ cup corn syrup
½ cup evaporated milk
2 cups butterscotch morsels

Beforehand Preparation

Toast cake slices; cut into 1-inch cubes. Shave chocolate. Chop nuts quite fine.

Tabletop Technique

At range in fondue pot, combine corn syrup and evaporated milk; bring just to boil over moderate heat. Remove from heat; add butterscotch morsels; stir until smooth. Transfer pot of sauce to fondue stand over low flame or candle. Serve a portion of cake, chocolate, and nuts to each guest. Swirl cake into hot sauce, then into shaved chocolate or nuts. 6 servings.

DESSERT MENU
Butterscotch Fondue
Spiced Tea

Caramel Snack Fondue

7 caramels
2 teaspoons hot water
2 cups popcorn
4 firm apples
Lemon juice
⅔ cup heavy cream
1 cup miniature marshmallows
2 tablespoons brown sugar

Beforehand Preparation

Place the caramels and water in top of a double boiler. Heat, stirring frequently until the caramels are melted and sauce is smooth. Pour over popcorn, and toss until well coated. Form into 16 tiny clusters. Peel apple; cut into bite-size pieces; brush with lemon juice.

Tabletop Technique

In fondue pot over low heat, combine cream, marshmallows, and brown sugar. Stir until blended and marshmallows are melted. Using heat-proof fondue forks, swirl apples and popcorn clusters alternately into hot sauce. 4 servings.

SNACK MENU
Caramel Snack Fondue
Lemonade

Chocolate Festival Fondue

½ pound seedless grapes
2 large oranges or other fruit
1 (8-ounce) package dates or other dried fruit
1 (4-ounce) package candied citrus peel
4 large brownies
1 teaspoon orange rind
1 package (8 squares) semi-sweet chocolate
½ cup milk
Dash cinnamon

Beforehand Preparation

Wash fruit; stem grapes; cut oranges, dates, and citrus peel into ¾-inch chunks. Cut brownies into 1-inch chunks. Grate orange rind.

Tabletop Technique

At range in fondue pot, combine chocolate, milk, orange rind, and cinnamon. Cook over low heat, stirring occasionally until chocolate is melted and sauce is smooth. Transfer to fondue stand over low flame or candle heat. Keep at an even low bubble. Add a little warm milk if mixture becomes too thick. Spear chunks of fruit or cookies on long-handled fondue fork and dip into pot; swirl to coat pieces. 4 to 6 servings.

MENU
Chocolate Festival Fondue
Demitasse   Cordials

Doughnut Dunk

Doughnuts cut into bite-size pieces (about 1 cup
    per person)
1 cup semi-sweet chocolate morsels
½ cup chunky-style peanut butter
¾ cup milk

Beforehand Preparation
Prepare doughnuts.

Tabletop Technique
In fondue pot over very low heat, melt chocolate;
blend in peanut butter. Gradually add milk. To
serve, dunk doughnut pieces into hot sauce using
heat-proof fondue forks. 4 servings.

DESSERT SNACK MENU
Doughnut Dunk
Soft Drinks

Fondue Café

2 cups freshly brewed coffee
1 (8-ounce) package cream cheese, softened
½ cup brown sugar
6 ounces Gruyère cheese, grated
¼ cup flour
Sugar wafers, lemon pirouettes, chocolate chip
    cookies

Beforehand Preparation
Prepare coffee. Blend cream cheese and brown
sugar. Grate Gruyère cheese; toss with flour.

Tabletop Technique
At range in fondue pot, heat coffee. Gradually
stir in grated cheese, stirring constantly until
smooth. Add cream cheese mixture, stir until
smooth. Transfer to fondue stand over very low
flame or candle. To serve, dunk cookies into fondue. 4 servings.

DESSERT MENU
Fondue Café
Demitasse with Brandy

Fruit Melba Fondue

1 (17-ounce) can peach halves
2 bananas
Lemon juice
1 pint vanilla ice cream
Chocolate sprinkles
Chopped nuts
Toasted coconut
1½ cups raspberry jelly
¼ cup red wine or water
2 tablespoons butter

Beforehand Preparation

Drain peaches; save juice for dunking or cooking; cut into bite-size pieces. Peel bananas; cut into 1-inch slices; brush with lemon juice. Stir ice cream to firm stage with fork; keep firm (not runny) in freezer. Chop nuts; toast coconut.

Tabletop Technique

In fondue pot over low heat, combine jelly, wine, and butter. Stir until smooth. Serve portions of fruit, ice cream, sprinkles, nuts, and coconut on sectional plates. Spear fruit on heat-proof fondue forks. Dunk into hot sauce, then dip into ice cream and nuts, toasted coconut, or sprinkles. 4 servings.

DESSERT MENU
Fruit Melba Fondue
Demitasse   Champagne

Fudge Frosting Fondue

2 oranges
2 large fresh peaches
1 pint fresh strawberries
2 tablespoons butter
2 tablespoons water
¼ cup light cream
Dash salt
¼ teaspoon almond extract (optional)
1 (12½-ounce) package fudge frosting mix
¾ cup miniature marshmallows
1 cup pecan and/or walnut halves

Beforehand Preparation

Peel and section oranges; cut each segment in half. Dip peaches in boiling water and slip off skins; cut into 1-inch cubes. Wash and hull strawberries.

Tabletop Technique

In fondue pot melt butter over low heat. Add water, cream, salt, almond extract, frosting mix and marshmallows. Cook over low heat, stirring constantly until marshmallows are melted. With fondue forks alternately spear pieces of fruit and nuts and swirl in sauce. If fondue becomes too thick, stir in a few drops of hot water. 4 servings.

DESSERT MENU
Fudge Frosting Fondue
Iced Mint Tea

Goodness Fondue

2 pears, peeled and cut into 1-inch chunks
2 cups pineapple chunks, drained
1 tablespoon lemon juice
4 (1-inch) slices pound cake
4 ounces American cheese
2 ounces Swiss cheese
1 tablespoon butter
1 egg, slightly beaten
1 cup milk
1 tablespoon sugar
½ cup coffee liqueur

Beforehand Preparation
Prepare fruits. Brush pears with lemon juice.
Dice pound cake into 1-inch cubes. Shred cheese.

Tabletop Technique
At range in fondue pot, melt butter; add cheeses
about 3 tablespoons at a time, stirring constantly
until smooth. Allow to cook for 10 minutes. Remove pot from heat. Stir in beaten egg; gradually
blend in milk, sugar, and coffee liqueur. Transfer
to fondue stand over very low flame or candle.
Alternately spear fruit and cake and swirl in hot
cheese-dessert sauce. 4 to 6 servings.

MENU
Goodness Fondue
Coffee with Lemon Peel

Mixed Dried Fruit Fondue

1 lemon
1 (11-ounce) package mixed dried fruit
2 cups Chablis
2 tablespoons brown sugar
¼ teaspoon cinnamon
Dash powdered cloves
1 (5¼-ounce) package fluffy white frosting
    mix
1 cup chopped walnuts

Beforehand Preparation
Grate lemon rind to make 1 teaspoon. Cut 1 thick end slice from lemon. In saucepan cover fruit with water; add lemon slice. Simmer for about 20 minutes or until fruit is plump but still firm. Drain; save fruit juice for a beverage. Combine wine, brown sugar, lemon rind, spices; simmer for 5 minutes; strain. Prepare frosting mix. Chop nuts.

Tabletop Technique
At range in fondue pot, heat wine mixture to boiling. Transfer to fondue stand over low flame. To serve, dunk pieces of fruit in wine until heated through, about ½ minute. Dip hot fruit into frosting sauce then into chopped nuts arranged on individual dessert plates. Add additional hot wine if mixture cooks down. 6 servings.

MENU
Mixed Dried Fruit Fondue
Brown-Edged Cookies
Espresso   Cordials

Mocha Fruit Fondue

½ pound ripe peaches
½ pound ripe sweet cherries
16 slices candied citrus fruit
4 (1-inch) slices pound cake
⅔ cup cream
8 ounces sweet chocolate
2 teaspoons coffee powder

Beforehand Preparation
Dip peaches in boiling water and slip off skins; dice into 1-inch cubes. Pit cherries. Cut candied fruit rounds into bite-size pieces. Toast cake; cut into 1-inch cubes.

Tabletop Technique
In fondue pot over low heat, stir cream, chocolate, and coffee powder with wooden spoon until creamy and smooth, about 5 minutes. Keep hot but not boiling over very low spirit or candle flame. With fondue forks alternately spear pieces of fruit or cake and swirl in hot mocha sauce. 4 to 6 servings.

MENU
Mocha Fruit Fondue
Coffee   Kirsch

Pears in Cheese Fondue

1 pound Swiss cheese
2 teaspoons cornstarch
1 tablespoon cognac
1 cup peanuts
½ cup sesame seeds
6 fresh pears
Lemon juice
1½ cups dry white wine

Beforehand Preparation

Shred cheese. Blend cornstarch with cognac. Chop nuts; toast sesame seeds. Just before serving, peel and core pears. Cut into bite-size pieces; brush with lemon juice. (Pears may be served, one to a person, to be peeled and cut into cubes at the table.)

Tabletop Technique

In fondue pot heat wine to almost boiling. Add cheese, about 3 tablespoons at a time, stirring constantly until smooth after each addition. Add cornstarch mixture; heat until mixture bubbles. Keep bubbling gently over low spirit or candle flame. To serve, swirl pears in fondue, then into nuts or sesame seeds. If fondue begins to thicken, add a little heated wine. 6 servings.

DESSERT MENU
Pears in Cheese Fondue
Little Sugar Cookies
Coffee   Sauterne

Peppermint Cream Fondue

    4 frozen patty shells
    Crushed peppermint candy
    4 small bananas
    Lemon juice
    ⅔ cup heavy cream
    1 cup miniature marshmallows
    2 tablespoons powdered sugar

Beforehand Preparation

Cut frozen patty shells into 6 wedges. Place on ungreased baking sheet. Bake at 400°F. for 10 to 15 minutes or until browned. Crush candy. Just before serving, cut bananas into 1-inch slices; brush with lemon juice.

Tabletop Technique

In fondue pot at range over low heat, combine cream, marshmallows, sugar, and candy to taste. Stir until blended and smooth. Transfer to fondue stand over low flame or candle. Alternately spear mini-puffs and banana slices on fondue forks. Dunk into fondue. 4 servings.

DESSERT MENU
Peppermint Cream Fondue
Coffee   Brandy

Pineapple Chocolate Crunch Fondue

1 cup crushed pineapple
1 cup semi-sweet chocolate morsels
1 (7½-ounce) jar marshmallow cream
Pretzel sticks

Beforehand Preparation
Drain and measure pineapple.

Tabletop Technique
In fondue pot over very low heat, melt chocolate. Gradually blend in marshmallow cream and pineapple. Keep hot over very low spirit or candle flame. To serve, dip pretzels into fondue. 4 servings.

SWEET SNACK MENU
Pineapple Chocolate Crunch Fondue
Hot Tea   Chilled Soft Drinks

Index